Elevate Your 8:

21 Days to Prosperous Time Management

Kris McPeak

Kris McPeak

SilverPeak Development

Copyright © 2018 Kris McPeak

All rights reserved.

ISBN: **9781720296126**
ISBN-13:

DEDICATION

This book is dedicated to Tammy Gocial and Colette Cummings, who, during my years at Webster University, taught me the activity that inspired this book. Thank you both for being such an inspiration to me during my career. I appreciate you both so much.

Kris McPeak

SilverPeak Development

CONTENTS

	Acknowledgments	i
1	Introduction	7
2	I'll Sleep When I'm Dead	13
3	You Work a 40 Hour Week for a Living	24
4	Sciences, Bitches!	35
5	Working for the Weekend	49
6	Elevate Your 8!	63
7	Making it Work	77
8	Appendix	
9	About the Author	

Kris McPeak

SilverPeak Development

ACKNOWLEDGMENTS

I could not have finished this project without the help and support of these amazing individuals:

Doug Ferguson, who gave me my first review on Amazon and continues to inspire and motivate me;

Lindsay Maloney, who gave me the confidence I needed to finally finish this project;

Allison Melody and J.J. Flizanes, who have provided so much education, support, and trail-blazing...when I grow up I wanna be just like you ladies;

Bobbi Abram, who mentors me in my day job and gives me room to grow, learn, and create;

The coolest husband in the world, Charles McPeak. You give me everything, even when I might not deserve it. I love you.

Introduction:
You Ain't Getting More Time Anytime Soon

"There are 24 workable hours in every day."

That is a quotation from 1995's EMPIRE RECORDS. Corey, played by Liv Tyler, has baked cupcakes for Rex Manning Day at the record store, in spite of being called a nerd by her best friend Gina, played by Renee Zellweger. We learn later that Corey takes speed and diet pills to keep her energy up because there was huge pressure from her father to succeed academically and get into Harvard. She also intends to throw herself at Rex Manning so she can lose her virginity.

And you thought you had problems. The good news is, Corey sees the error of her ways and gets the boy by the end of the movie.

So, yeah, there ARE 24 workable hours every day, but that doesn't mean you need to work yourself to death. And even though Liv Tyler is gorgeous and smart and adorable, we also know that speed, and diet pills doesn't keep us in good health or good spirits.

And Rex Manning really did have an awful haircut. But Gina had sex with him anyways (sigh). It was payback for that Killer Tomato thing.

Then there's American Idol Season 8 Winner Kris Allen, whose catchy "Live While We're Dying" gives it all to us in seconds:

Looking at the hands of the time we've been given here
This is all we got then we gotta start thinkin' it
Every second counts on a clock that's tickin'
Gotta live like we're dying oh
We only got 86 400 seconds in a day
To turn it all around or to throw it all away
Gotta tell 'em that we love 'em while we got the chance to say,
Gotta live like we're dying

Converting the hours to seconds, we have every day; it sounds like a lot. I don't think I could even count to 86,400 without getting frustrated and bored. And I don't really spend my day counting the seconds. They do count for sure. But we will group them in hours for this book because, well, I can't count that high.

Productivity expert Laura Vanderkam, who I will quote later in this manuscript, wrote an exceptional book called, "168 Hours: You Have More Time Than You Think." Her challenge? Think about a 168 hour week rather than a 24 hour day. Her strategies are similar to mine when it comes to logging and setting priorities. When you are finished reading this book, you should make sure you check hers out (But only AFTER you finish this book).

Yes, it's true: we still have 24 workable hours every day. We need to use them accordingly, or we are going to impede our ability to enjoy our time. Time is seriously one of our most precious commodities. Someday you might get more money at work, earn more vacation time, or win lottery. But none of us will figure out how to squeeze 25 hours into a day. Whoever invents that process is going to make a whole lotta chedda! Hopefully, by then someone will have figured out how to actually "Beam Up." Seriously. If Mike Teevee can travel by television, then surely we can Beam Up (Willy Wonka reference, sorry to the younger souls who never knew the wit and wisdom of Gene Wilder).

That didn't end well for Mike Teevee, though. Bummer.

But I digress.

Time Management is neither a skill nor a strength. It's a process. Our issues with time management vary according to our life patterns. One week we might be killing it at work and finishing project after project; and the next week we can't sleep, can't focus, can't finish anything. It ebbs and flows. It is impacted by our life events, our health, our family and friends, our jobs, our hobbies. Sometimes it feels as if it's completely out of control, and sometimes it feels as though we've mastered the monster.

No one wants to admit that they struggle with time management. But we are easily distracted by outside influences, we don't feel like we have enough time now to do what we need, and we don't finish what we start. Our failure to acknowledge and control this process is slowly killing us. We are reactive, we procrastinate, and we can't say no. The Department of Statistics at the University of Wisconsin-Madison states, "In this era of downsizing and the quest for efficiency, businesses of all sizes are asking employees to take on extra tasks to boost productivity."

A 2015 online article in the Business Insider claims, "Checking emails at home is just part of the job for most

Americans, who would also prefer to receive money rather than more paid vacation or sick days, according to a poll." Meanwhile, lunch breaks are getting shorter, 60-hour work weeks are commonplace, and 34% of Americans don't take their vacation days. All of this means that we need to take a better look at how we are spending our time.

What I've come to realize in my 20+ years working in higher education is that time is precious, and there are so many things I want to do and experience before my life ends. And when I was told by a previous supervisor that "expecting" to work a 40 hour week in that position was unrealistic, I put my foot down and said, "NO MORE." These days, I come from a mindset where I want to sleep 8 hours each night, work only 8 hours per day, and maximize my time on the weekends. What that tells me is that I have 8 nebulous hours daily from Monday through Friday. I have a chance to utilize an additional eight hours each day for "stuff" on the weekends. It's what I'm calling **Elevate Your 8.**

Only 8 hours a day? To do all those things on my to-do list? You have got to be freaking kidding me.

No, I am not kidding; and YES you can get all that shit done.

And it's easier than you think! I was inspired to write this book after putting 8 and 8 together and realizing that I only need to manage 8 hours daily and 16 on the weekends.

Get your 8 hours of sleep each night to fulfill your need to rest.

Work your 8 hours a day to maintain your work and life balance.

And then prioritize the things you need to do and what to do with those other 8 hours, while delegating or scheduling your most significant projects and greatest social opportunities on the weekends.

You are going to rethink your attitude towards time and the specific resource it is. You are going to identify the most important things you want to accomplish on a daily and weekly basis. And you are going to come up with a plan to completely kick ass and take names with those 72 hours you'll have to hang around.

And that's what this little book is all about. Let's get started!

Before we can work on that negligible 8 from Monday through Friday, we need to take a peek at your current daily habits. You are going to spend one week tracking your sleep and one week doing a time-on-task at your place of employment. You are going to write down EVERYTHING you do during the day outside of sleep and work. And you are going to write down everything you want to do on the weekends to ensure that you are returning to the office on Monday feeling relaxed, recharged, and ready to tackle any task for the week. There are many surveys and studies reinforcing the notion that employees feel more engaged and productive when they aren't exhausted. I guess that you bought this book because

a. You need more sleep
b. You are struggling with work/life balance
c. You don't think you have enough time to get everything done

Don't worry - we are going to carefully observe all your habits and tasks in line with your goals and passions. And hopefully, by the end of this journey, you'll have a plan in place that will maximize the Weekly 8 hours and Rock Your Weekends.

Fo' Shizzle

Chapter 1 - I'll Sleep When I'm Dead

Till I'm six feet under
I won't need a bed
Gonna live while I'm alive
I'll sleep when I'm dead
'Til they roll me over
And lay my bones to rest
Gonna live while I'm alive
I'll sleep when I'm dead
--Bon Jovi

In many ways, this song is an awful example to use, because Jon Bon Jovi still looks fantastic even though we know that man didn't sleep during the 80's whatsoever. However: we need sleep every night. Good solid sleep. Sleep that rests our bodies and our minds. Sleep assists our memory. It curbs your appetite. It helps us live longer and decreases the risk of certain diseases.

Several scientific theories hope to explain why *we sleep* and why we NEED sleep.

There is the **Inactivity Theory** - suggesting that "inactivity at night is an adaptation that served a survival function by keeping organisms out of harm's way at times when they would be particularly vulnerable." So, don't move and stay away from the dark, so you don't get eaten.

Next up is the **Energy Conservation Theory**, suggesting "the primary function of sleep is to reduce an individual's energy demand and expenditure during part of the day or night, especially at times when it is least efficient to search for food." Our body temperature and caloric demand are reduced when we sleep, which supports the notion that we need sleep to conserve our energy resources.

The **Restorative Theory** maintains that "sleep provides an opportunity for the body to repair and rejuvenate itself." There are studies which prove that necessary body functions like muscle growth, tissue repair, and protein synthesis occur mostly during sleep.

A recent theory has to do with changes in the structure and organization of the brain - this is known as **Brain Plasticity Theory**. While not entirely understood, it is becoming clearer that sleep plays a critical role in brain development of infants and young children.

You can discover and ead more about these theories at http://healthysleep.med.harvard.edu/healthy/matters/benefits-of-sleep/why-do-we-sleep

With all this science backing up the importance of sleep…why do so many people deprive themselves?

There are many, many reasons.

We think that we don't have enough hours in the day to get things done. Because we are overworked anyway and can't embrace better work and life alignment, we force ourselves to stay up late or get up early to get things done. Some of us completely waste our time on social media, television, and video games. We choose socializing, chores, eating, working our day job, and time-wasters over a good night's rest.

I once knit an entire scarf in one night while watching two Billy Wilder movies. On a work night. Why I did this, I'll never understand. I didn't even wear the scarf the next day. But I guess I really wanted to finish it. And it was only the tenth time I'd watched "Witness for the Prosecution" in about two weeks. Maybe it was the movies. I love Billy Wilder's films.

We may even be so stressed, sick, and overly medicated that our 8 hours of sleep are not quality hours. And this defeats the purpose of sleep.

There are a plethora of resources out there for how to improve your sleep, and my favorite one is the book "Sleep Smarter" by Shawn Stevenson. I will quote him several times in this chapter. His book is useful, funny, contemporary, uses science to make points and pop culture to drive those points home. I chose to purchase the Audible version of his book since Shawn reads his own work as well. Beyond what you will learn in this chapter, I highly recommend getting your hands on this book. You will absolutely not be sorry.

Through all my research I learned that there are several easy things we can do to take back our nights and get better sleep. Even just instituting one or two of these recommendations can move you closer to fulfilling the first Full 8: **Fall Back in Love with Sleep!**

Reduce Caffeine

Caffeine is a stimulant and can prevent you from getting a good night's rest. It is found in coffee, tea, soda, some candies, and some weird places like yogurt and protein bars. I'd been taught as a young adult that eating Plain M&M's can provide a good shot of caffeine if you are traveling on the road and need to stay awake. I'd also been told that Mountain Dew has the most caffeine than any other carbonated beverage. All I know is, when I have more than one cup of coffee in the morning, I'm jittery for a while; if I have a Diet Coke with dinner, I'll have a hard time getting to sleep.

Who's old enough to remember No-Doz or Vivarin? When I was a Resident Advisor in college, we used to get "Good Stuff" boxes at the beginning of the school year that had Vivarin pills in it. Seriously. Shaving Cream, Deodorant, tampons, condoms, bad snacks and Vivarin. I only pulled an all-nighter one time during my five-year undergraduate pursuit which was the only time I tried Vivarin. Big mistake. Huge. I felt horrible for days. So there you go.

According to Sleep Education, the average daily consumption of caffeine by adults in the US is about 300 mg per person. This is about three times higher than the world average. No wonder we have issues sleeping! Between coffee shops, soda, and energy drinks, this stimulant is everywhere.

Sleep Education's website goes on to say, "Caffeine begins to affect your body very quickly. It reaches a peak level in your blood within 30 to 60 minutes. It has a half-life of 3 to 5 hours. The half-life is the time it takes you're your body to eliminate half the drug. The remaining caffeine can stay in your body for a long time." Yikes. Now I know why the Diet Coke nags me if I have it at dinner. To keep caffeine from disrupting your sleep, don't have any caffeinated beverages after 2 or 3 pm.

Carey Lawson, an Executive Director of Advancement from Eunice, Louisiana, attributes eliminating caffeine at 3 pm to her sleep wins. Phoebe Chiang, a Los-Angeles based Event Planner, knocks off the caffeine at 4 pm and is ready for bed after 9 pm.

Consider Effects of Other Beverages

While some people do pass out after consuming too much to drink or partying hard, alcohol is generally not something that can help you sleep. A 2013 article in Psychology Today states, "Alcohol consumption, in excess or too close to bedtime, diminishes the quality of sleep, often leads to more waking throughout the night and lessens time spent in REM sleep and slow wave sleep in the later part of the night, the deepest and most restorative phase of sleep." Alcohol is considered a depressant, but the immediate effects of alcohol can act as a stimulant – this is called biphasic effects. To engage in a better night's rest, cease your alcohol consumption at dinner and don't drink too much before bed.

Reduce your Evening Entertainment

I used to be one of those people who "absolutely needed" the TV on to go to sleep. What this wound up doing for me was waking me up in the middle of the night, noticing that I didn't like what was on the tube, and changing channels. And that usually meant investing 30 or so minutes into whatever I chose. But even if you have no television in your bedroom, even checking out that new episode of "Scandal" before bed can keep you awake. The Huffington Post cited an article that stated 68 percent of participants watched TV for more than 55 minutes, the two hours leading up to bedtime — precious minutes that could be spent sleeping. To minimize TV interference, DVR your must-see shows and tune in earlier in the evening or on weekends.

So reading is better than television before bed, right? Not necessarily. Engaging in novels or stories that are scary, overly emotional, or high energy can raise your blood pressure and heart rate, which makes it harder to sleep. Eva Kennedy, a higher-education administrator in San Francisco, makes sure she turns off her television early and reads in her living room while listening to what she calls "good music." Depending on the day and her mood, this could be soft country music or classical music. Most of the time, the music she chooses has limited songs, "so I normally fall asleep before all the songs finishes playing."

Your Phone

Uh, yeah, I'm definitely going there. I actually wanted to avoid this too. Because I have been one of the worst culprits. Mobile Phones are the world's biggest blessing and curse. On the one hand, we can be so much more productive using our phones because of all the handy-dandy apps and gadgets...but there are many scientists and medical folks who believe that phones do not belong in the bedroom.

An article in the US Today stated, "To fall asleep, your body needs an increase in a hormone called melatonin. The problem is, a backlit phone or tablet decreases melatonin production." This can lead to some tossing and turning in the bedroom. If you are an iPhone user, then you know that Apple introduced the Night Shift feature on their phones which reduces the back-lit blue lights to a warmer tone that can minimize the disruptions. There are also glasses you can purchase that will reduce the amount of blue light your eyeballs are taking in.

There is also a major concern with the radiation emitted by wireless phones and their antennas. The National Cancer Institute has an entire fact sheet dedicated to this. Some of the details include, "Cell phones emit radiofrequency energy (radio waves), a form of non-ionizing radiation, from their antennas. Tissues nearest to the antenna can absorb this energy." If you are concerned about this, read articles about it and look for other places to store your mobile phone at night. I was fortunate enough this year to attend a retreat where we were asked – expected though – to turn off our cell phones and tablets during the sessions. It was quite liberating to know that I didn't have to have my phone on and in my hands constantly. And I also learned at this retreat about alarm clocks that simulate the sunrise according to your sleep and wake schedule. So I bought one. Total game changer. You set your wake time and choose from several "waking" tones; then the clock will start to light up 30 minutes before your wake-up time. This is meant to wake you gradually and comfortably. It's awesome.

Bedroom Conditions

The National Sleep Foundation has some fantastic resources on sleeping disorders and other sleep-related topics. Their "Inside Your Bedroom" section of their website is quite useful.

For example - how many times have you awoken in the middle of the night and had night sweats or were otherwise uncomfortably warm? That's because our body temperature rises and falls during the day; the natural dip of our body temperature can be affected by warmer temperatures. NSF recommends a bedroom temperature of around 65 degrees for optimal sleep. But if you or your significant other find that temperature to be too cold, there are bed liners you can purchase that will keep your body temperature from getting out of control while you sleep.

Light and darkness affect our sleep. Too much light makes your body think that it's still daytime and you should be up and mobile. Our body needs a dark room to relax into sleep. This is one of the reasons why shift-work is so awful for us – for night shift workers to get the best possible sleep, one literally has to blacken out the windows and doors to keep the room dark. In Shawn Stevenson's book he shares that shift work has been classified by the American Cancer Association as a 2A type carcinogen, grouped with nitrates, nitrites, anabolic steroids, lead compounds, and consumption of red meat (and the longest list of chemicals I've seen in a long time. I couldn't even pronounce most of them).
Artificial light at night can also trigger the brain's production of melatonin, making it harder to fall asleep and stay asleep.

I've started lighting candles in our house in the living room about two hours before bedtime so that we can still see to walk around the house, but we don't have to have too much of artificial light turned on in the house that could disturb our sleep later. Plus it makes the house smell nice. Bonus.

Changing your sheets is just as much about sleep quality as it is about hygiene. The smell of fresh sheets is pleasing and can aid in our sleep quality. The National Sleep Foundation recommends washing your sheets once a week, and sprinkling baking soda on sheets and mattress covers, then vacuuming. Choose a laundry detergent with a pleasing scent and make sure you aren't allergic to it.

Once again, in "Sleep Smarter," Shawn Stevenson dedicates an entire chapter to creating Your Sleep Sanctuary. He suggests things like blackout curtains, house plants, and removing all devices from the bedroom. And then…only use your bedroom for sleep and sex. I think I can live with that.

Exercise

"I'm not a morning person" is the reason I hear most often on why my friends don't work out in the morning. Most of them are runners or gym rats. With the advent of 24-hour fitness facilities, we can stretch our days to the point where we are hitting up the elliptical at 2:30 am.

And this practice is not suitable for us. First of all, if your adrenaline from a workout is up and charging, it's going to be a while before your body wants to go to sleep. Secondly, remember that our bodies were not engineered to be up 24 hours a day. So when it's dark outside, we should be sleeping. Which is why the energy you get from either an early morning workout or noon-ish workout is the best for maintaining a stable, regular sleep schedule. The energy and metabolism boosts get you through the day, and it allows your body temperature to get back where it's supposed to for sleep.

Heidi Sheaks, owner, and stylist at West Coast Cuts and Colors of Woodland Hills says that swimming every morning before work ensures that she gets a good night's sleep. "I used to be an insomniac," Sheaks reports. "I did not realize that a daily routine of morning swim exercise not only helps me sustain the work day, but I find I can actually fall asleep at night." A study by Kelly Glazer Baron from Northwestern University agrees with her. While other forms of exercise can stress our bodies, "Swimming can break that cycle both mentally and physically. Sensory deprivation, a complete lack of stress on the body, stretching, fat burning, muscle building, weight loss, combating depression, all of these powerful aspects of swimming are sure to help you sleep more soundly."

<u>New Parents</u>

While I'm not a parent, I've heard the stories.

"How's the baby? How much sleep are you getting these days?"

For new parents, figuring out the sleep schedule so the newborn gets all his or her due attention can be tricky. Stephanie Hilten, Director of Advancement for Carl Sandburg College, has a set system for tending to their newborn at home. She states, "Since we are opposites – he is a night owl, and I'm an early bird - after we complete whatever household chores that need to be finished after dinner, he plays Xbox and I go to sleep...usually around 8 or 9 or 10. Then he lets me sleep until 11 and watches our son sleep on the baby monitor while he plays Xbox. This allows me time to get a few good hours before we move our son into our room and he comes to bed. It works for us because we both get whatever hours we need and still sleep in bed together, something we believe is important in our marriage." So there is definitely an argument for X-Box...for new parents.

WEEKENDS AND SLEEP

I want to talk a minute about the Weekends. Many people have very different patterns of work-week sleep and weekend sleep. Do any of these sound familiar?

*Stay up late on Friday because you know you can sleep in on Saturday

*"catch up" on sleep Friday and Saturday nights

*Sleep so late that you miss your morning meal

It's an "American malady" according to an article from CBS News. In the United States, we tend to make up our sleep time over the weekends. But for that to actually work, it needs to be an hour-for-hour make up. So, for example, if you lost five hours of sleep over the course of a week because of your job or other emergencies, you need an extra five hours of sleep on the weekend - which isn't really Elevating Our 8. Just Sayin.

CHAPTER 2 - YOU WORK A 40 HOUR WEEK FOR A LIVIN'

Unless you were born into money, or you won the lottery, or you're like Jules in PULP FICTION, and you're gonna "walk the earth," – like Kane in Kung Fu - chances are you have to go to a job daily to support yourself or your family.

The blog page Trans4Mind discusses several differences between your job and your vocation. Jobs aren't always liked. You have predefined working hours and a set wage. Jobs don't always align with your personal values. And you will eventually be fired, quit, or retire from your job.

Vocations, on the other hand, are literally defined as callings. Your vocation means you are doing things just right and you are in the field that fuels your passion. You will never retire, you're your vocation. You enjoy your weekends and anticipate the beauty that is Monday when you return to your calling. You feel happy all the time because your work is a natural expression of YOU.

So which one sounds better?

In my first book, "Making 'Work' Work for You," I outline several strategies and hacks to help yo9u manage your job should you be struggling with your current 9 to 5. The book's sections are divided according to my experiences through 20+ years of work in higher education. I don't want to duplicate that book here – that would be silly. But I will highlight a few things you can think about when it comes to those 8 hours every day when you physically go to a place of employment and earn your living.

Generational Differences

I fully identify with my Gen X self, and I value work/life balance and flexibility above all other values in my workday. Most of my former supervisors were Baby Boomers; my parents were of the greatest generation. My father, in particular, taught me about persistence and dedication, but he also encouraged me to live life to the fullest. A former Boomer Supervisor told me that working 40 hours a week in my current position was unrealistic. I've had supervisors remind me to take a vacation, while others turned my requests down and judged my requests as not being "reasonable." Who takes vacation to go to a film festival anyway?

Boomers focused greatly on loyalty and putting in hours to get ahead. A 2006 article in the Chicago Tribune stated, "For them, the best way to achieve was to become the workaholic generation." Which at times made things very difficult for us Gen X'ers who were ready to go to happy hour or hit the gym. I mostly bring this up to remind you that generational differences affect us in the workplace. If you think your values are being challenged by a supervisor of a different generation, talk to him. Tell him your thoughts and concerns. Try to negotiate a middle ground – but don't be pushy. We will cover this in a later section.

How Did I Get Here?

Not all of us knew what we wanted to do right out of high school, or even right out of college. Many of us fell into our professions because of some of the involvement we had in college. That's exactly how I found myself working in higher education. In college, I was a Resident Advisor in the residence halls for 2 ½ years. When I realized I could get paid real money to do this for a living, I literally geeked out. Can I make door decorations and plan parties and get paid for it? Yes, I'm in.

Since then, my path has been rough at times, but still rewarding. And there finally came a time where residence hall work wasn't good for me anymore. I switched to another field in higher education, one that is very different from college housing.

You may have a similar story - a job in high school or college led to a career once you received the proper training. Or maybe you found a job that was exciting when you were 24, but there were not enough opportunities for advancement. Therefore, you've been on a lateral path ever since then. Even worse – you took a job because it came with a regular paycheck and now you curse that decision on a daily – god forbid, even hourly – basis.

Whether you are thanking the Universe for landing you in the right place, or biffing yourself on the head a la Special Agent Jethro Gibbs because of your foolish decision, all of us challenge our vocation from time to time. This is not only normal; it's healthy. Life events, relationships, and all sort of other outside factors can affect our daily 9 to 5, even when we do our best to shelter them from each other.

But you should be honest with yourself. Yeah, you gotta make a living; but according to Dolly Parton, you gotta make a life, too. Don't let yourself suffer in a position that is slowly sucking the life out of you or driving you to drink. Check the appendix at the end of this book for my online courses that can help you rethink your career and search for your Dream Job.

Tricks for Getting Through...

Picture this: you've decided to gut out another year at your current gig... or, it's just absolutely the busiest season for you and your colleagues...and you find yourself grasping at straws, sleeping poorly, and eating crap. You need some tips and hacks for reimagining your work day.

For example - don't let your calendar run amuck over you. Control it. Keep it clean and tidy. Schedule lunch every day and schedule travel time between meetings. Ask your assistant to block project time for you on your calendar – or, better yet, do this yourself. You'll get so much more work done in those work blocks; you'll forget how grumpy you are because of how productive you've been!

Looking at this another way - do you like your colleagues and supervisor, but the work itself is not sustaining your passion? Maybe it's time to have that conversation you're your supervisor, let her know that you need a challenge. Ask her if you can take on some more projects, maybe things that align with your Talents and Strengths (purchase StrengthsFinder 2.0 to learn more about this strengths thing. It's VERY cool).

And dammit, you need to take a vacation! This isn't just some random benefit that HR dangles but hopes you never use. Vacation and time away are crucial for regeneration and further engagement in your place of business. A 2015 article in The Guardian states, "Researchers at Oxford Economics hired by the US Travel Association put the numbers [unused vacation time] at about 169 days, equivalent to $52.4 billion in lost benefits." That's 211,250 days of vacation left on the table to die. Pathetic.

But why? Some people want to show their loyalty, and not taking vacation is a possible way to do that. Another quotation from The Guardian, "We are the only industrial county that does not mandate vacation days and 25% of our workers receive none of them at all."

It is, however, a top-down practice. Employees who see their supervisors take vacation are more likely to do the same. So, if you supervise others, make sure you take your time off. And if you don't supervise others, make sure you take your time off. For realz.

Attitude

As Arvind Devalia says on Lifehack.com, "Remember, you are more than your work." Let your soul and spirit define how you approach your job or vocation rather than letting the job define you. Plus, unrealistic expectations on what you "should" be doing in your life (from parents, family, friends, supervisors) can be frustrating. Devalia also suggests contributing to a productive workspace and pleasant work environment as much as possible. Don't gossip. Don't carry your dissatisfaction around like a big rock on your shoulders. If your attitude is positive and optimistic, that can be a happy influence on your peers and colleagues. Charles J. Alaimo from Huff/Post so wisely has said, "Your perspective will determine your reality."

Geoffrey James from Inc.com writes about ways you can improve your attitude at work. Some of these are obvious, but others sort of hit me upside the head. For example, "Use setbacks to improve your skills." Of course! This is how we learn and grow. It doesn't always have to be during our annual review or performance appraisal where we figure out how to improve in our job. Rather than getting defensive when a colleague doesn't like our project idea, ask yourself: "Maybe I could have presented it differently." Or, "I should learn more about her perspective." This also allows you to go within and find any blocks you are having that made you feel negatively in the first place; if you can identify those and just work on yourself, you won't be pointing the finger at the other guy all the time.

Okay - I know what you are thinking. All this stuff about tips and hacks and attitude is really great. But it doesn't change the fact that I work 12 hours a day. I can't work only 8 hours a day. I can't get the work done. I can't put myself at risk at work.

What is all this "can't" crap?

Kathy Caprino from Forbes Magazine writes this about overtime and overworking (April 30, 2015):

1. Employees often believe that working for longer hours means they'll get more done.

2. As managers arrive at the office earlier and depart later each day, their employees will mimic their schedules because they believe working long hours is necessary to gain approval.

3. Employee-fostered culture often dictates that those who work longer hours are going to be promoted more quickly for "working harder."

4. Employers do not effectively communicate work-life expectations, so employees default to prioritizing work over life outside.

5. Finally, managers don't have complete visibility into each employee's workloads, so they continue assigning additional work without considering existing projects and responsibilities.

If you are a manager, these five points can help you plan and prioritize your day as well as how to support your team with their work. As a manager, it's your job to role model that work/life balance to your team (if you are a manager who doesn't believe in work/life balance, this is probably the wrong book for you. Sorry).

What if you aren't a manager? How do you tell your boss that you have too much work or that you prefer to go home at 5 pm and this is why...? For many of us, this can be a daunting and frightening task. We may feel nervous about speaking up; and yet, if no one advocates for you, you must advocate for yourself.

Kyle Lee from The Muse outlines some great suggestions, and I agree with all of them. The bottom line is you have to approach your supervisor with patience and respect and speak from a place of appreciation and honesty.

Problem Solve: to reduce your workload and get back down to the 8 hour day, you need to be able to solve problems and not be whiney or complain. For example, talk about how you can complete this specific report or project in a shorter amount of time and why you believe it can be done. Or, share your ideas on how your Staff Meeting can be shorter and more productive for everyone.

Be Specific: generalizations aren't going to help you here. You have to outline the specific issue and provide a particular solution. You can't just say, "There's too much to do, and I don't have time." Instead, say, "my current workload for this quarter, which includes eight financial reports and four evaluations, seems unrealistic with my current meeting schedule." Then propose the solution.

Focus on the Future: you want to be strategically future-oriented because you can't change the past. You will need to provide a resounding argument (not a fight, mind you) on how your future performance will be improved by making these changes you are requesting. For example, "if I can take a small 15-minute break in the morning and afternoon to get outside and walk around, my head will be much clearer, and I can get focused back on my project."

Or, "if the administrative assistants can all stagger our lunches, there will always be coverage at the front desk, and no one will have to be stuck here while everyone else is at lunch."

Aaron McCoy from Idealist Careers also suggests leaving emotion out of the conversation, express concerns about quality, and convey your appreciation for the opportunity to share your ideas. You can't be emotional in a situation like this because it decreases your credibility. Your manager may instead decide you shouldn't have the position at all! Sharing how the quality of your work will improve the specific changes you suggest will impress upon your supervisor that you care about creating a sound, quality product. And you must say thank you. Appreciation of the time is essential to recognize. Your supervisor may be much, much busier than you are. Treat that opportunity to discuss your concerns as a gift.

Sadly - you might do all this work and provide the most amazing and convincing reasons why your workload and work hours should be reduced you're your work/life balance you're your boss can still say "toughen up." Or, "this is the job you've accepted."

Well, poop.

Now what?

That's a situation that will take some additional soul searching beyond the scope of this book. But given that I've been there myself, here are some options:

a. Look for another job
b. Go back to working long hours
c. Work more efficiently at the office with your co-workers.

I continuously go back to this notion. When a proposal was put in front of me as the supervisor or manager and the employee seemed convinced that it could be done, why not give it a try? I feel as though managers need to listen to their employees and treat them as members of a team, not serfs in the kingdom.

My hope for you, should you choose this road towards Work/Life Balance, is that you have a supervisor or manager who is a true mentor and leader.

I want to deviate from the current conversation and introduce an exciting time management tool that is the office version of the "Four Way Win" that we will describe in Chapter Five about weekends. Jeffrey B. Harrington, MBA, from California State University-Chico has an incredible strategy for both taking a work break and doing networking. It's what he calls "Network Naturally." Or, in other words, "leave your desk behind and talk to people." When Jeff was in his first professional position after college, he worked as an Assistant Hall Director at a mid-size California university and developed what he calls a "career leveraging" practice in his day to day work routine. His Daily Networking Walks became a popular skill that he honed in his Blah blah blah year's living on campus, and he continues to practice this in his role as an Admissions Counselor.

Jeff's tips:

- *Physically get out of the office. If you need an excuse to leave your department, go buy some coffee or a snack.*
- *Go the long way to the bathroom on a different floor and pass the desks of people you don't know well. Genuinely say "hello" as you pass.*
- *Personally, hand-deliver something to a colleague's office that doesn't need to be hand delivered.*
- *Stop by a nearby office instead of writing ten emails back and forth to solve a problem. People appreciate the effort.*

Next Up: we are going to start tracking your habits and behavior and prepare to Elevate That 8!

Chapter 3 "Science, Bitches!" or - How To Conduct Your Own Personal Experiments

This chapter is going to prepare us to make the necessary changes in our not-as-negotiable Eights: Work and Sleep. If we want to make the best possible use of our Other Eight, we are going to have to do a great deal of planning, observing, and recording. You need to dedicate yourself to this project if you are going to make any changes in your life and maximize those eight hours.

Yup, if you thought this book was just going to be like one of those lecture-style presentations from your professional seminars where you just listen and don't engage – WRONG. You're going to do the work, and you're going to engage. It's the only way you're going to see change, okay?

Make a promise to yourself right now that you will dedicate the next three weeks to learning and identifying all your habits and redefining your priorities. Go ahead….

(go to https://www.krismcpeak.com/elevate8book **to download your promise)**

Now that you've made that promise to yourself, we will go ahead and get started. While the idea behind this book is to figure out how to dominate those OTHER eight hours, first you have to figure out exactly how you're spending your time at work and during your sleeping hours.

Seriously – if you don't think you can dedicate the time to these exercises over the next 14 days, then put this book down and check your calendar. Come back to the book when you know you can commit to the assignments and activities. I will not be offended.

Assignment #1

You'll need to go into these next few exercises as if you are experiencing your downtime for the first time. You also need to assume that you already work only 8 hours a day and sleep 8 hours each night. Don't worry – after you've done the exercises, you can make adjustments to your time segments if necessary. I do know that many people can operate just fine on just 6 hours of sleep while others need 9 or 10 hours. We will reconcile this later.

For two weeks, you are going to keep a sleep journal and a Time on Task Journal. Ideally, do the Work Tasks the first week and then do the sleep journal during the second week. The reason I don't want you commingling your journals and assignments is that I really want you to focus on the trends you notice in your work days and sleep patterns at different times. If you try to do both sections in the same week, you may give up on the task entirely, and we don't want that. Or you may be overwhelmed with the task – we don't want that either. This book contains all the notes you need, but you can download all the worksheets and handouts at my website.

WORK

Let's do our work day first. Start the "ticker" with the minute you unlock your office or turn on your computer in your cubicle. You're your journal and write down the time. Then every time you witch activities, you'll write down a new start time and go from there. And don't skimp on the minutes or the interruptions. LIST. THEM. ALL. Including you're your cubicle neighbor wants to talk to you AGAIN about the Series Finale of SCANDAL. We need to identify potential time wasters, when you are most productive, and how you are using your time most effectively during the workday.

I'm pretty lucky, and I don't mean to rub anyone's noses in it, but here's what one of my days looks like:

7:45 am Arrive at Office and start the computer

7:50 am Put away lunch, use the restroom, and get water

7:55 am Open Outlook and take a quick peek at my calendar

7:56 am Close Email

8:00 am Work on Scholarship Reviews

10:00 am Go for a quick walk around the block

10:10 am Process Donations in online software

10:30 am Meeting with Staff

11:30 am Work on Report for President

12:30 pm Lunch Break

1:30 pm Open Email and Respond to messages

3:00 pm Go for a quick walk around the block

3:10 pm Refresh water and use the restroom

3:15pm   Respond to voice mail messages

3:45 pm Check on meetings for tomorrow - close Outlook

4:00 pm Clean Desk and Prepare tasks for the next day

4:30 pm Leave for home

It looks pretty simple, yes? Truthfully, I've paired my routine here down to a simple group of tasks that I may complete in a day – but what I want you to see is the structure of it all.

I'm a morning person, so reports and projects that require immediate focus and attention are done in the morning. I like to take a slightly later lunch break because it makes the afternoon go by faster. The afternoon is when I respond to voicemails and emails. I have made it a priority to get my production done when I have the most energy. In that sense, I'm making sure my assignments and my day to day projects are completed. If some emails or voicemails are urgent, those folks will find a way to call me or find me.

I have spent a good amount of years figuring this out for myself, and it's not a perfect system. Right now, however, it really does work for me. Five years ago, when I was asked to do a Time on Task for a previous employer, my journal looked a little something like this (ugh):

7:30 am Go to the office and turn on the computer

7:45 am Check Email and respond to voicemail

7:59 am Answer incoming call from your parent

8:20 am Return to answering emails

8:45 am Quick meeting with Administrative Assistant

9:05 am Walk to Starbucks with a colleague

9:35 am Return to email

10:00 am Senior Management Meeting

12:30 pm Return to email (yes, this is already getting old)

12:45 pm Lunch Break

1:15 pm Campus Police Meeting

2:30 pm Upset student waiting for me upon my return

3:15 pm Finish conversation with student and follow up with supervisor

5:00 pm Check email one last time and, provided there is not a student or staff member waiting to talk to me, go home

And I'm generous to myself here. Most of the time it was constant interruptions that did not fall into increments of ten or fifteen minutes. It also didn't count the days that I stayed late to, you guessed it, catch up on email. Which is why I had to change my email protocol when I changed careers. I needed to take back control of my day and do my work when I am most productive.

Your TIME ON TASK forms are available at https://www.krismcpeak.com/elevate8book

When you've completed your Time on Task assignment, go back and read all your pages multiple times. Check for themes. Consider these questions when you are identifying themes in your workday:

a. When are you getting the most work done?

b. When do your meetings tend to be scheduled? How many meetings are happening each day?

c. Who seeks you out for questions or concerns?

d. How often do you spend time with your supervisor? Your supervisees?

e. How much time do you have for your lunch break?

f. Do you get sucked into "water cooler conversations"?

g. What other trends do you notice within your workday?

Now - put these journal sheets away, because we are going to work on our sleep for the next week.

SLEEP

Your sleep journal should sit on your bedside table so you can write in it soon after you wake up. If you need to do your business first – or let your dog do his business first – or turn the coffee maker on…go for it. But try to hit up that sleep journal as soon as possible after waking.

You are going to record answers to the same questions every day for seven days - and, yes, including the weekends. Your sleep journal pages are available at https://www.krismcpeak.com/elevate8book

When the week is up, look at your themes and patterns.

1. How many nights out of 7 did you sleep through the night?

2. How many nights of the 7 did you dream?

3. How did your morning feelings shift or differ over the 7 days?

4. On the nights you woke up in the middle of the night - what seemed to be the average amount of time before you fell back asleep?

5. Did you notice any other trends or themes from your week of sleep journaling?

Assignment #2

You've done a ton of research (that's the "Science, Bitches! part). It's time to make sense of it all.

This is not going to be easy - in fact; you are going to want to throw your journal pages across the room every few days or so. Please don't. You will need them. You are going to analyze your unproductive work habits and sleep habits and make tiny little changes until you can comfortably equal out to 8 and 8.

There are worksheets on my website that are going to help you identify the habits that need changing and then formulate the habits you want to create. I'll explain them first, and then you can go to work. Find those worksheets at https://www.krismcpeak.com/elevate8book .

You can start either with your work journal or your sleep journal - but just work on one at a time.

Similar to Robert's Rules of Order with discussion - you share a pro, then a con, then a pro, then a con, until you have three pros or three cons in a row. So it will be with your habits and themes.

The Work Journal - go through one at a time and identify good work habits and poor work habits. Here are some examples:

Good Work Habits - Pros	Bad Work Habits - Cons
I take a lunch break every day.	I can't leave the office at 5 pm because I want to clean out my email.
I don't open my email until I return from lunch.	If "Susie" my co-worker comes into my office, I can't get her to leave until she's talked about SOMETHING for at least 10 minutes.
I take one break in the morning and one break in the afternoon.	I schedule too many back to back meetings.

Keep on going until you have your three good or three bad habits in a row.

If you finish up this exercise ending with three good habits – well, that's awesome! You have less to work on than you thought! If you finished with three poor habits, then you'll have more work to do after all. But don't worry – we will get you there!

Take all of your Cons - Poor Work Habits. Rank them in order from the most to least offensive. This will be your priority list for creating new, positive habits.

Now - look at your Pros - Good Work Habits. Do any of those Pros help you to erase a Con?

For example: one of my good work habits is taking breaks, one during the morning and one during the afternoon, I take a quick walk around the block. But one of my bad work habits is opening up the internet and drifting from the productive, working reason why I went online in the first place, Because most likely it was not to get sucked into Facebook or my Gmail Promotions. I can't just keep the browser closed, because I have a work task to perform. So, I will get up and take my walk. Then I'll return to my desk and get right to the online task I need to complete. I've used that time that might have been wasted on frivolous web-browsing and reset my environment. I return to my web task feeling refreshed and ready to concentrate.

See how that worked? The bad habit of needless web browsing was cleared by the good habit of taking a walking break.

If you aren't able to clear a Con/Bad Habit with a Pro/Good Habit, don't worry. These are lucky instances and usually fun bonuses you will find that save you time with this project.

Look at your Most Offensive Bad Work Habit. You're throwing up a little in your mouth, aren't you? It really bothers you that you do this. Go rinse your mouth out, and let's analyze this bad boy.

Let's take the example from the chart above. In that example, your co-worker, Susie, barges in your office and lingers for roughly 15 to 20 minutes to talk about "stuff." This really isn't a bad habit, but it does distract you, and you wrote it down for a reason. How can you mitigate this scenario so you can be more productive?

a. *Is Susie and acquaintance or a Vital Work Friend?*
b. *Does she linger to talk about work-related things or personal things?*
c. *Do you find yourself interested in what she's saying? Or are you bored all the time?*
d. *Does she leave on her own, or do you have to tell her to go?*

Depending on your answers to these questions, you may take different approaches.

If Susie is your Vital Work Friend, then you have the opportunity to talk to her directly so you can remain friends but be more productive. Let her know that her visits are always appreciated, but they block your "workflow" and can be distracting. Suggest that you go to lunch or coffee once a week to catch up.

If Susie is just a work acquaintance, share with her that you have an important project to work on and you'll come visit her later. Let her know that you really want to learn more about this or that, and then get up from your desk as though you were going to walk her out – or, better yet, tell her you have to use the restroom. When you return, close your door.

Bad Habits or unfortunate situations like these can be challenging to manage when other people are involved. And you may have dug yourself into a Workplace Con/Bad Habit without even realizing it. It's much easier to let the practice continue then possibly hurt someone's feelings. In the grand scheme of things, perhaps this co-worker could also use the discipline because she comes to your office to avoid a project or phone call that seems to occur around the same time as her visits.

Here's another example. You are consistently late to a standing meeting across campus because you don't schedule travel time into your schedule. The meeting you have prior is always a favorite of yours because of the topic or committee; it could be anything. But you can't be late anymore – the chair of that standing committee has started complaining about your tardiness to your boss. Therefore, a new habit or practice could be to find a better closing time for the previous meeting and scheduling the appropriate travel time to ensure that you are on time. This is a simple matter of what? Controlling your calendar.

Habit change can be hard; I'm not kidding around there. But since you've identified now what needs work, you're going to feel a whole lot better once you develop strategies later in this book.

For now, let's relax a little and get ready for the weekend.

Chapter 4 - Working For the Weekend

I had a fun time searching for meaningful quotations to start off this chapter. Because this weekend stuff sort of flies in the face of my argument that you spend 8 hours working, 8 hours sleeping, and 8 hours of other stuff. But – we don't go to work on the weekends. Ideally. Maybe we do work on the weekends, but our "weekends" are Tuesday and Wednesday. Regardless - I think you know what I mean. Whether your weekend is the traditional Saturday and Sunday or whether it's something else, we all have some form of Weekend to reckon with.

In the sense that The Weekend can be an entirely different beast, we approach these two days – Saturday and Sunday – as a total of 32 nebulous hours of potential productivity, to-do-list completion, social and hobby time, or …dare I say it…"nothing" time (remember, you're still going to sleep your regular 8 hours during the weekend). There is a rationale for all these various ways to spend our Weekends. Depending on your current situation, you may have different approaches on different weekends.

Mom and Dad with three kids are going to approach the weekend quite differently than, say, me and my hubby. The Family of Five may have birthday parties to attend, soccer games to watch, museums to visit, or best friends to hang out with.

My hubby and I might have copious amounts of laundry to finish along with swimming or triathlon brick practices to plan. The single career woman who isn't dating anyone might go for a pedicure with her girlfriends and then meet up with her sister for a margarita. Our priorities are going to be different, and that's totally okay.

To make this first section a little more fun, I've developed some strategies with each of the fun Weekend Quotations I referenced earlier. Well, actually, I made up those strategies. Sue me; this is supposed to be a fun part.

This will get you warmed up and ready to work on that Weekend Productivity!

I have never in my life found myself in a situation where I've stopped work and said, 'Thank God it's Friday.' But weekends are special even if your schedule is all over the place. Something tells you the weekend has arrived and you can indulge yourself a bit.

--Helen Mirren

Ah, Helen Mirren. She makes just thinking about weekends sexy and sophisticated. Surely, at one point in her life, she might have looked at her watch and was ready to bolt out of the office by 4:55 pm. Maybe?

Weekends are Special, she says. Weekends are for indulging yourself a bit. Preach on, Helen!

What does that mean, then? You take your weekend time - or a portion of your weekend time - to do something special for yourself. Or your family. Or your significant other.

That pedicure mentioned above? Great example.

Going to the movies by yourself and theater jumping so you can see two in a row? Of course.

Surprising your kids with a visit to Magic Mountain? You bet.

Going for a 12-mile training run and going out for pancakes with your running buddies. I love it.

These sorts of plans aren't going to necessarily check off items on your to-do list, but they are a chance to participate in something you love to do with people you'd love to be with. Or just spoil yourself. We'll refer to this Weekend Activity as "Indulgence."

☆☆☆☆☆☆☆☆☆☆

You know what I want to do? Wake up one weekend and not have to go anywhere and do nothing.

--Derek Jeter

Don't we all feel like this from time to time. My husband and I run a non-profit swim and triathlon team, and there are at least 2-3 competitions or training activities every month...which usually means one or more of the weekend days is scheduled. I love our team and our business very much, but every now and then I'm just thrilled to be able to say, "we have no social or team obligations this weekend. None!"

From time to time, you will have weekends where you can absolutely afford to do nothing. And I'm here to tell you that's a good thing. Straight up relaxation and downtime. If you have a porch, do some porch sittin'. Do you have a hammock? Hang around in that hammock. Dogs? Take them for long walks. You really have nothing else to get done, so enjoy it!

Don't let the perfect be the enemy of the good. Lower the bar. Actually spending ten minutes clearing off one shelf is better than fantasizing about spending a weekend cleaning out the basement.

--Gretchen Rubin

Oh my goodness! I want to make this so much more of a mantra for me! If you read the previous weekend quote, you've learned that I'm pretty busy on the weekends. Sometimes I don't want to do a full house cleaning, like my hubby would like to do. I want to do the floors and laundry and maybe see a movie. This is the person who wants to get everything they can out of the weekend – household chores, fun, and relaxation. Amen!

I recently finished a couple of audiobooks from Sarah Knight (Get Your S*it Together and The Life-Changing Magic of Not Giving a F*ck). I guess you could call her a Productivity Anti-Guru. She calls herself that, anyway. In her books, she talks about choosing two essential cleaning tasks that take no more than an hour and cycle through those daily or weekly. For example: on Friday evening I might clean the bathroom and fold the laundry. Then on Saturday afternoon and I can wash all the sheets and wash the living room floor. Then on Sunday afternoon I can change all the linens and dust the bedrooms. See what I mean? I think Sarah Knight is pretty brilliant in that regard. I highly recommend her books.

"Hands up if you're ready to do something you'll regret this weekend. Go forth! You have my blessing."

— **Florence Welch**

Uh oh. Is there going to be some debauchery in your future weekend? Is someone having a bachelorette party or a karaoke night? Or maybe you're going to do some day drinking at home while playing Cards Against Humanity with your neighbors.

As college students, many of us had weekends filled with parties and drinking and hookups and otherwise bad decisions. And you know what? I think we all need to have at least one or two of these in our lives. Because in some ways, it's the release we can sometimes need from the daily grind and our routine weekends. But I have just two rules about this: Plan Ahead, and Be Safe.

If you already know that you are going to be consuming copious amounts of alcohol at your weekend debauchery event, make sure you already have a designated driver arranged, or agree with your friends that you are going to Uber it home. Don't risk an accident or an arrest because you didn't plan ahead. I don't know about where you live, but the DUI laws in California are pretty strict. It's not worth the risk. So that is a major part of planning your

Throw Down Weekend Event.

I'm quite sure i sound like a mother hen or your college RA right now. And I don't mind that because in many ways I am both (at least, I WAS an RA in college). But this book is all about ELEVATING your additional time, not deflating it. A bad night out that features a negative ending is DEFLATING.

"It's not that we spend five days looking forward to just two. It's that most people do what they enjoy most on those two days. Imagine living a life where every day is your Saturdays and Sundays. Make every day your weekend. Make every day a play-day..."

— James A. Murphy, The Waves of Life Quotes and Daily Meditations

This is definitely more of a State of Mind quotation, I think. I love what James Murphy has to say about "most people doing what they enjoy most" on the weekends. Why does it have to be that way? Saving up a little of your Eight Hours during the week can definitely include what you enjoy most.

Take me for example. My current Joys in Life are swimming and knitting. Well, I tend to swim on the weekday mornings (part of that Elevated 8); about three days a week I am working on a knitting project during my lunch hour. So I cover a little bit of those things constantly rather than only the weekend.

Making everyday a Play Day is more than just a state of mind.

It takes discipline, scheduling, and a little bit of self-love and self-care. You aren't doing yourself any good if you put off all your fun things and good feelings until Saturday and Sunday. That makes you a grouch for the full week, and you won't be any good at work, at home, at the gym, etc. Your colleagues will be bummed out when they are around you, and your significant other will suddenly be working late every day this week. Am I right?

☆☆☆☆☆☆☆☆☆☆☆☆☆

"Although I understand that all days are equal with 24 hours each, most of us agree that Friday is the longest day of the week and Sunday the shortest!"

— D.S. Mixell

If this is your sentiment, then you probably spend all week thinking about Friday, and when you get to the end of the day, you have no idea what the hell you are going to do WITH your weekend. You've just been waiting for it to happen. By Sunday at lunch, you have your rhythm, but oh crap - you have to go back to work tomorrow. This is the person who needs to do more weekend planning ahead of time, rather than just looking forward to it. No Loverboy song here - "Working for the Weekend" needs to be "Getting Ready for the Weekend."

☆☆☆☆☆☆☆☆☆☆☆☆

Do any of these various Weekend Profiles sound like you? Maybe you are all of them, depending on how you approach your weekends. Because all of these weekend attitudes and scenarios can be appropriately utilized at any given weekend. Probably not all at one time, and probably not the same ones every weekend.

That's where my Quadrant Planner comes in (hang in there, it's coming soon!).

Weekend Strategies

Fast Company published a fantastic article from productivity expert Laura Vanderkam on her 10 tips for making the most of your days off (Fast Company, January 2, 2013). Included in her tips are planning, but not filling every minute; make sure to exercise, but DO schedule downtime, and don't do too many chores or work every minute. I think her suggestions are super helpful and easy to utilize. In fact, her philosophy does link up well with my Quadrant Planner.

Ms. Vanderkam also channels the late Steven Covey in a second article from Fast Company dated January 2, 2012. Here's what she says:

"In The 7 Habits of Highly Effective People, the late Steven Covey calls this 'putting first things first.' He suggests an exercise that involves thinking of roles that matter to you. I'm a writer, a wife, a mother, a runner, a friend, and a volunteer as the president of the board of directors of the Young New Yorker's Chorus. If your list of roles starts getting unwieldy, you could compress them into the major categories: career, relationships, and self (which includes exercise, hobbies, and anything that moves your soul). Then think of your top two or three priorities in each area that you'd like to accomplish over the next 168 hours. Block these priorities into your calendar first. Once you do this, you'll likely notice something. First, blocking six to nine priorities into

a 168 hour week still leaves a lot of blank space. But second, if you accomplished all those things, you would have an absolutely amazing week."

This is a great way to plan and ensure that you are not just doing chores and checking email during your weekend. Categorizing the things you need or want to achieve during the weekend (or the entire week for that matter) according to the various roles you play and their importance keeps your eye on the ball and avoids the downward spiral of the unplanned Netflix Binge or the Happy Hour that goes on too long. Plus, it ensures that no one gets left out.

Stephanie Hilten, who we talked about in the sleep chapter, has a very firm grip on her weekend and the roles she has to play. She told me, "NO WORKING! Now, that isn't always possible, so I try to take time off the following week to make up for a day I work on the weekends for an event if I am able. I check emails because I'm an administrator and am required to be available at all times BUT I only respond if needed or late at night when it isn't taking away from my family."

Hilten has made some particular choices about her weekend knowing that, in her field, the occasional weekend event is going to crawl in from time to time. In Entrepreneur Online, Dorie Clark wrote on how to be productive, occasionally include a work-related event, and still have a fun weekend. From the article published on November 14, 2014, she talks about personal priorities as well as professional goals. She shared an example of Stephen King, who writes on the weekends. Which is okay, because he made a choice to write every day. Nothing wrong with that. And I love the section where she discusses Stew Friedman's books "Leading the

Life You Want," which identifies four key spheres of life: family, friends, work, and community/health. Dorie writes:

"He advises professionals to look for a "four-way win," which is the quest for activities that help fulfill us on multiple levels (even if we can't reach all four simultaneously). We only have so much time in the day, and we can't do it all. But if we combine activities, we can fit more in. Want to work out? Invite your husband or wife to join you. Need to attend an event for the charity you support? Try to get your friends involved so you can maximize the impact and socialize with them, too. Getting creative about blending these aspects of your life can help ensure you have more time to spend on the things you care about."

This takes double-dipping to a whole new level, one that actually feels good!

My husband and I have been able to work on this a little. We both work on managing and running our non-profit swim team, which includes swim meets and competitions.

So while we are encouraging and coaching our team (work), we are also spending quality time together (family), and getting in some exercise when we compete (community and health). If you count the fact that we've made friends with many of our swimming colleagues and socialize with them outside of swimming, I just shared with you a Four Way Win! Huzzah!

FINALLY – The Weekend Quadrant Planner

Okay, I've been referring to the Quadrant Planner for a while now. This is a little gem I somewhat "invented" when my hubby and I lived in Chicago. It's so simple and easy that it's practically stupid.

It really is kind of stupid – but it was my weekend lifesaver for several years. Let me give you some background here…

During our Chicago years, I was still a very avid movie-goer back then, and I also ran a Wednesday evening karaoke show at the bar my husband managed. Crunching in some of the things that needed to get done on the weekends and get in two to three movies on Saturday or Sunday was quite the undertaking (seriously – I did this pretty much every weekend for about five years.)

Originally, the Quadrant Planner was just a blank piece of paper folded in quarters, and I drew lines over the folds to create four quadrants (similar to Covey's Time Management Grid or the Johari Window). Those quadrants would be labeled as follows:

Movies
Chores
Errands
Money

Movies – this is where I would write down the movies I wanted to see, and then check my Chicago Reader or the web to find out where they were playing and could I do a 2 or 3 movie day at one theater. To some of you, this may seem like THE most ridiculous thing ever. But at that stage of my life in my life, seeing movies was one of the most important things to me. It deserved a hallowed place in my weekend. And when I planned ahead and scheduled it, I could easily get in 2 or 3 movies in a day at one theater. Don't judge me.

(Hmmm...planning....surely there is a point here....)

Chores and Errands kind of go together – what needs to get done around the house (laundry, cleaning, etc.) and what needs to get done "in town." Stuff like:

1. Grocery shopping
2. Pick up prescriptions
3. Toiletries
4. Dry Cleaning
5. Hardware store

My fourth quadrant says "Money." For me, at this period in my life, money was still an issue. The karaoke show that I did on Wednesdays provided some extra cash for me, so that would get parceled out on the weekends. If I had $100 available, how did that get appropriated?

Movie Money (duh).
Groceries
Other Errands
Party or Play Money

Writing it all down made it real, and it gave me a weekend budget that I could live with and use to stay on track. Which in itself has nothing to do with time management, but there's something to be said about a weekend budget, especially if funds are sparse. And this philosophy will kick in a little later when we start talking about time as currency.

NOW – these days, the quadrant would look a whole lot different. Given my current interests, responsibilities, and living situation, my Weekend Quadrant might say this:

Exercise and Movement – these days, getting in some exercise is really important. We mostly swim during the week, so on the weekends, I tend to take our dog on long walks (40 minutes or more) and attend at least one class using my Class Pass (of which I am a huge fan, speaking of productivity things).

Biz Things – between the swim team and running my personal brand (SilverPeak Development), are there events, tasks, or planning that has to be done? We may be attending a swim meet or having a function for the team. There might be an organized bike ride or a race that we need to attend in support of our team. There might need to be a podcast recorded or a blog post written. Or the monthly newsletter might need to be produced for the swim team.

Errands and Chores – these are pretty much the same as before, only in this situation, they are combined into one space on the quadrant. It seems that lately, I do more of the errands and my hubby does more of the chores, but that also greatly depends on the weekend and what's going on. If he's not doing work on the house, he does more chores. If he is, then I step in to do laundry or clean the kitchen and bathroom, etc. I enjoy errands much less than I used to, so the quicker we can get these things done on any given weekend day, the better!

Social Responsibilities – now that we are older, we enjoy doing way more social things with other married couples. There is a small core group of us who tend to do some things together like going to dinner, having brunch at someone's house, doing fun little outings like Watermelon Festivals and July 4th Parades.

I don't see very many movies in the theater anymore. In fact, I do this almost never. I miss this sometimes, but I also really like my life the way it is. I find it fascinating that our priorities change as we grow older and/or make changes in our vocation or hobbies.

And there are some weekends when I don't even touch the Weekend Quadrant Planner. Those weekends roll out organically, and we go with the flow. Think back to that Derek Jeter quotation about getting to do nothing. Exactly. How cool it can be just to wake up when you want and let the weekend tell you what to do.

Chapter 5 - Elevate Your 8!

Welcome to Your Future. Or at least, the part in the book you've been waiting for! You have done a great deal of work to get to this place, and we've made it our main goal of this book – figure out how to make the best use of the remaining 8 hours of your day, plus weekends.

Let's recap:

1. You learned more about the importance of sleep and how you can make each night's sleep more effective in your life.

2. You explored an overview of the workplace and why it's so critical to keep your work hours to 40 per week (8 hours per day). You considered how you came to find your current gig in the first place and how you might make the days more palatable if you aren't in a position to seek new employment.

3. You participated in a 14-day study of your sleep habits and tracked all of your daily tasks at work. From there, you found themes in your behavior and determined where you need to make some habit or priority changes.

Now - let's Elevate Your 8!

Let's do a little math first. Sorry. You can probably even do it without a calculator (not gonna lie, I needed the calculator).

For the work week - you have 8 hours a day multiplied by 5 days a week: that's 40 hours ("You work a 40 hour week for a living, just to send it on down the line." -Alabama. Sorry, had to do that).

For the weekends - we already subtracted your sleep, so you are left with 32 hours over Saturday and Sunday to structure and schedule.

40 + 32 = 72

Now you have 72 hours to play with in order to do all the other cool things you want or need to do. Holy crap – that's like <u>**THREE FULL DAYS!**</u>

I could honestly end the book now and just tell you to get over saying you don't have enough time – because with the math alone I've proved that you do. But that would be a cop out, and I have so much more stuff to share. It's gonna be fun, too! When you realize all the cool things, you can get done with all this extra time. What a gift. What a blessing. What a freaking surprise! Or, if you're Marisa Tomei in "My Cousin Vinny," - What a fuckin' nightmare!

In a previous chapter, I shared with you some strategies and philosophies on how to prioritize those extra hours. One included defining all the roles that matter in your life (wife, mom, volunteer, etc.) and then prioritizing the tasks for each role. The goal here is to finish high priorities first and on down the line.

The second strategy suggested that you should try to overlap your activities to include all the important people in your life (Family, Friends, Work, and Community/Health for the "Four Way Win"). And by all means – if you are connecting with either of those strategies, give them a try and see how they feel. While these two procedures were written initially to get you through the weekend, they are unquestionably applicable for the work week as well. While these two procedures were written initially to get you through the weekend, they are definitely suitable for the work week as well.

Throughout this chapter, we are going to look at some short definitions and identify attitudes about time that will help you to Elevate Your 8. As we do this, there will be some exercises you can complete to help move you in the right direction.

You checked out your sleep habits and your work behaviors to get a sense of what you need to do to get both of that area back to a maximum of eight hours. Now we are going to analyze how to spend those THREE FULL DAYS (also known as 72 hours).

Which means you have more math and brainstorming to do. Thinking outside of your sleep and work activities, what the hell else do you do?

Exercise
Walk Your Dog
Eat
Write a Book
Journal
Meditate
Spend time with Family
Spend time with Friends
Take care of your Kids

"And So Much More!"

Here's what my Activities Sheet looks like (and it's mostly in order of when I do them)

Morning Routine (which includes breakfast, meditation, journaling)

Swim Workout (which includes commute, workout, shower, and commute)

Dog Walking - Swim Meets - Yoga - Shopping - Laundry – Other Chores

Admin Work for Side Hustle #1 (which includes my swim team and those various activities)

Admin and Creative Work for Side Hustle #2 (which includes writing this book and working on SPD.com

I guess my example is not the easiest because, in addition to my day job, I have two side hustles. And my weekends are totally contingent upon what those responsibilities are. So I'm a good example for those of you who are Type A Personalities and want to do everything.

On Swim Meet Weekends, that's pretty much all I do. Wake up, get dressed, pack the car, travel, set up the tent, be a cheerleader, compete, break down the tent, and so forth. But swim meets happen roughly 1-2 times a month, so I adjust accordingly depending on what the weekend brings for me.

If my husband is working on the porch (lately, that's a very big IF), and wants help painting, I might help him for 2-3 hours in addition to doing laundry and other domestic things. I might also have a few mystery shops to do (I LOVE these – they really do exist!), so I'll have to bug out for a couple of hours while he continues to work on that porch. He also hates to shop so I don't feel guilty about this at all.

The point being - those 56 hours fluctuate from weekend to weekend and evening to evening. Knowing what you like to do, what you have to do, and how long it takes to do it will help you budget, so your time is spent well and not wasted.

What's all the talk about spending, and waste, and usage, and currency....?

Here's my attitude –

TIME IS MONEY!

Sorry for the "all caps" and what appears to be a shouting match on my end but I wanted to make sure you heard my attitude completely. Time. Is. Money.

What does that exactly mean? Basically time is a currency in that we only have a finite amount of it and we can't just create or add more time. So we have to spend that time - that currency, if you will - in the most creative and frugal ways as possible to ensure that we have enough of it to attain our goals, engage in our hobbies, make a living, and spend time with our loved ones. Dictionary.com lists this statement as a Cultural Definition: "time is a valuable resource, therefore it's better to do things as quickly as possible."

The present form of the expression seems to originate in a speech made by Benjamin Franklin in 1748, but the sentiment is much older. The saying 'the most costly outlay is time' is attributed to the 5th-century BC Athenian orator and politician Antiphon.

For the purposes of these exercises, we are going to address units of time in terms of currency. Money. Cash. Benjamins. Chedda. Whatever helps you think of it as a finite resource that you have to spend carefully and intentionally? Elevating Your 8 is really just smart budgeting if you think about it.

Break down the idea of hours and minutes into chunks of Time Currency. You have cash and bills that are in various denominations, yes?

Let's think of our time in some of these chunks, okay?

10 hours (which you'll really only use on the weekends)
5 hours
2 hours
1 hour
(if you must) 30 minutes

So your Time Currency is going to be spent using those chunks. When you identify an activity that requires your time, assign it a currency. In order to spend our time wisely, we need to get a sense of how much time we spend doing all of our daily activities.

I referenced my swim workouts earlier. Where those are concerned, I "spend" the following:

20 minutes to the pool
60 minutes IN the pool
10 minutes to shower and dress (yes, I'm that quick)
20 minutes to work

That's just about two hours. I would list all those things together as "Swim Workout" and assign it a currency of two hours. That gives me a little wiggle room if there is more traffic on the way to work.

I also have what I call a Morning Routine (lots of people have one, I didn't coin the term). It in itself fluctuates day to day, depending on a few things. But generally speaking, this is what I'm doing Monday through Friday once I wake up - the first glimpse into those 8 I'm gonna Elevate:

3:50am - wake up (I'm a swimmer, remember?), weigh myself, use the ladies room

4:00am - make coffee for the hubby and wake HIM up (I'm a super nice wife)

4:05am - retreat back to the living room and meditate

4:15am - do my Morning Pages

4:30 am - work on Side Hustle #2

4:50 am - Eat Brekkie

5:00 am - finish packing swim bag and dress for the pool

5:30 am - leave for the pool

That 3:50 am throws things off since it's a 10-minute increment, so I'll dump that and just say that my "Morning Routine" is 90 minutes - 1.5 hours.

If you put together my morning routine and my swim workout, I've spent 3.5 hours so far.

I've got 4.5 hours left.

I need to work my evening commute into there, so assuming traffic is decent, that's 30 minutes. I also enjoy walking my dog after work - he loves his "Momma Time." That walk is between 30 and 45 minutes. Then, dinner. About 45 minutes once we both eat and do the dishes.

Are you keeping up? I'm at 6 hours.

TWO HOURS LEFT? How is that possible?

I'm thrilled to have two hours left. This means I can do any of the following things before I put my head on the pillow for my 8 hours of sleep:

I'm thrilled to have two hours left. This means I can do any of the following things before I put my head on the pillow for my 8 hours of sleep:

*work on business stuff
*watch a TV show or movie
*knit
*sex (hey, a girl's got needs)
*pack the swim bag for the next day

*pack lunch for the next day
*grocery shopping (see explanation below)

Most of these things are on my activity list. Some are not, so I need to add them. And from where I stand, there are no real time-wasting activities here. Some may consider the TV show to be a time waster, but I do enjoy my entertainment and not totally ready to give that ALL up. I don't do three movies a day anymore, but I still like my shows.

So I have now navigated an average Monday through Friday pack of 8 hours. I'm feeling pretty good about the standard "work week."

How did YOU do? Did you run out of time? Did you have too much time? Look at your "budget" of 8 hours and switch some things around.

But what do you remove or add? You saw how I added activities to my extra two hours. I looked at some activities that were part of my general enjoyment and side businesses and looked at what I could get done in two hours. If I choose the movie or the TV show, that's probably going to be the entire time. And I COULD pack my swim bag while I watch a movie. I could also knit while i watch a movie. If I choose the business, I could spend one hour on each biz; or 30 minutes on each biz and then knit for an hour. I consider myself lucky - I have time left, so I have options.

Cutting activities to save your time is not easy. I know this. I've been there before. Part of Elevating Your 8 is setting priorities and identifying "must do" and "can do" activities.

Happy Hour with your co-workers? Maybe that's just a "Can

Do."

Your son's soccer game? Probably a "Must Do."

Is it your night to cook dinner? That's a "Must Do." People are counting on you!

Going out for ice cream afterward? Probably a "Can Do." How much time do you have left?

Laundry? Okay, this is a good thing to kick around for a second. Are you out of underwear or socks? Is your Swim Team T-shirt still dirty and hasn't been washed in a week (this is a HUGE problem in my house). Maybe take two minutes to peruse your closet and make sure you have the clothing and accessories you need for the next day.

Grocery Shopping? I brought this up earlier. Another thing to kick around. Are there ingredients for dinner? Breakfast? Kids' lunches? YOUR lunches? My hubby and I have a weird habit about shopping, and we mostly only shop for two or three days at a time. One reason is because we buy a lot of produce, so we always want fresh things. But he may also have private swim lessons, meaning we may fend for ourselves. Or he may text me at 3:30 pm to say, "I'm making chicken for dinner, and I want to have potatoes with it. Can you bring home potatoes?" So between the two of us it could be a "Must Do" every other day, but a "Can Do" otherwise.

Look at your activity list and come up with some priorities. Use the work you did in a previous chapter about what's most important in your life. Let that help guide you through the 40 hours from Monday through Friday. Because we are hitting up those weekends next.

WEEKENDS

Look at your activity list and come up with some priorities. Use the work you did in the Weekends chapter about what's most important in your life. Let that help guide you through the 40 hours from Monday through Friday.

There are also worksheets available from my https://www.krismcpeak.com/elevate8book

What about weekends? I have two thoughts:

1. Double your daily budget

2. Work in the "Can Do" activities that you don't get to during the week.

If you budget one hour to play with your kids Monday through Friday, then double that to two hours a day. Supplement if you find you have extra time.

You cut your happy hour plans with your colleagues - can you schedule some hangout time with them on Saturday or Sunday?

I don't mean for this to sound overly simplistic - but it's not all that difficult. And you have the Weekend Quadrant Planner to help you work in the really big things if you choose to use this tool.

Planning, Planning, Planning. Budget, Budget, Budget.

Time Is Money. It works, doesn't it?

21 Days?

The subtitle to this book is "21 Days to Prosperous Time Management." You can probably understand now what I mean by "prosperous", but what's this 21 days stuff?

You have already spent two weeks surveying your work and sleep habits. You came up with new habits to make the most of those 8 hour chunks and keep them at 8 hours. The remaining seven days are going to include planning your General Time Budget; and when those 21 days are through, you should be ready to Elevate Your 8. **But how?**

Earlier in this chapter, you created your Activities List, consisting of the things you Must Do and Can Do during your work week. You looked at how much time it takes you to do these things. Similar to how you budget your paycheck every week or every month, you are now going to create that time budget.

Use the grid at https://www.krismcpeak.com/elevate8book and plot in those budgeted items for each work day, and then work through the weekend. The Weekend Planning Quadrant can be your guide for Saturday and Sunday if you prefer.

I thought it might be fun to borrow from Ramit Sethi's

"Conscious Spending" idea. And by the way, his blog posts and books are highly entertaining and helpful, too - even for us non-millennials. Here's what he has to say about conscious spending from a blog post on his site, www.iwillteachyoutoberich.com:

1. Conscious spending is about making a plan on how you want to spend your money.

2. Most of us are not spending consciously—we're just spending whatever and then getting the bills at the end of the month.

3. Why should we spend consciously? If your plan is forward-thinking, you'll be able to pay yourself first by automatically saving/investing part of each dollar that comes in. You also won't feel guilty when you go out, or buy shoes, or whatever, because it will be an explicit part of your goals. And if you structure your system to pay yourself first, in a few months, you'll start to see it add up. Imagine where you'll be one year from now.

You wouldn't blow all your paycheck on shoes and drinks and iTunes purchases and THEN pay your bills, would you? Hell no. Ramit would go nuts! So why are we spending our time the same way?

So use your Activities List Worksheet and then jump on the grid and budget away! This is going to be so much fun!!

**SIDE NOTE:* in her book 'Get Your Sh*t Together", Sarah Knight provides a handy dandy downloadable workbook that includes an exercise called, "Things I did that weren't on my to-do list to procrastinate doing things that were." She challenges you to fill in the blanks, and then shares ten of her own. You want to be really clear on those things that you wind up doing in your 72 hours that maybe don't *need to be done in lieu of something else more pressing.*

Chapter 7 - Making It Work

To improve is to change; to be perfect is to change often. – Winston Churchill

If you do not change direction, you may end up where you are heading. – Lao Tzu

Everyone thinks of changing the world, but no one thinks of changing himself. – Leo Tolstoy

I share these quotations with you at this point in the book because these 21 days are meaningless if you don't do anything about it, right? And you did buy this book for a reason (not just that you are my friend or anything like that).

Face it you guys - you are going to need to make some changes.

And real change takes time.

You have spent 21 days learning about your habits, determining your priorities, and creating a plan for making a change and spending your time wisely. In the same way that it can "hurt" a little when you tighten the purse strings and try to spend less money or save more money, these time adjustments may hurt a little, too.

Don't. Give. Up.

Before I started working on this book, I facilitated a Time Management Challenge with my subscribers. One of the lessons included finding an accountability partner. Or partners. I think this is so incredibly important.

First of all - sharing your new priorities and goals with someone you respect and care for will make it easier to navigate the new horizons. When you want to fall back into the old, less productive habits, your partner can help you stay the course. When you are making it work, but struggling to do so, your partner can encourage you and tell you how great you are doing.

Secondly - having a partner means that you are getting your changes out there. You are letting people know what you are trying to accomplish. There's definitely something about making your project public that holds you to make it happen.

In Anna Newell Jones' book, " The Spender's Guide to Debt-Free Living," she talks specifically about this regarding going on a "spending fast" in order to change your habits. And it makes complete sense. When you "announce" on Facebook or other social media platforms that you are making a grand change in your life, people will respond to this, and they will want to know how you are doing. As you finish these 21 days, you may choose to make this grand announcement. Or, just stick with your accountability partner(s). But tell SOMEONE. Or you may find yourself backsliding to those old, bad habits.

Next, you are going to want to track, reflect and explore all your new, positive habits that allow you to Elevate Your 8. There's a Habit Tracker on my website:

https://www.krismcpeak.com/elevate8book that can assist you in taking your new habits to new levels. Again, this is something you'll do for 21 days. Pick one of your new, positive habits to track and fill out the form. Which habit did you choose?

Reflecting and exploring are a large part of ensuring that those habits stick and that you can see and feel the difference they are making. That's why I recommend journaling so much. If one of your proposed new, positive habits was to take a lunch break every day, then start exploring how you are going to do that. Put it on your calendar. Great. Think about where you'll take that break and what you will do with the time. Then after you've taken your lunch break on Day One, track it, and then reflect on it. Where did you go for lunch? Or, if you ate lunch in the breakroom, what did you eat? Who did you eat with? What did you talk about?

Writing all this stuff down may seem trivial, but I'm trying to get you to FEEL what it's like to have these new, positive productivity and time management habits. When you associate a feeling with your changes, you're much more likely to stick with it. Especially if that feeling is empowering and positive.

But what happens if you hate your new habit? If you try it for, say, five days and you're just not feeling it yet?

Well - like we said already - it takes 21 days to make a new habit stick. So ride out the 21 days first and see what happens.

Like any new process or procedure, you're going to want to

evaluate it once you start doing it. Again, stick with the journaling. Identify what you don't like about your new habit, and come up with other options. Find a solution to the problem by possibly tweaking your habit, performing the task in a different way. This isn't something your supervisor or partner has asked of you; you came up with this idea yourself. Trust yourself. Trust the work that you've done over the last three weeks. And give yourself a break. Change takes time.

But you don't have to take just my word for it....

On 99U.com, Gregory Ciotti writes this about creating triggers for new habits:

"Creating sticky habits is far easier when we make use of our current routines, instead of trying to fight them. The concept of if-then planning is built around environmental 'triggers' that we can use to let us know that it's time to act on our habit. Also known implementation intentions, this tactic involves picking a regular part of your schedule and then building another "link in the chain" by adding a new habit.

For instance, instead of 'I will keep a cleaner house,' you could aim for, 'When I come home, I'll change my clothes and then clean my room/office/kitchen.' Multiple studies confirm this to be a successful method to rely on contextual cues over willpower. So the next time you decide to 'eat healthier,' instead try 'If it is lunch time, Then I will only eat meat and vegetables.'"

Blogger James Clear has made a career out of creating and sharing his tools for habit change. He shares this formula on making habits stick:

Reminder (the trigger that initiates the behavior)

Routine (the behavior itself; the action you take)
Reward (the benefit you gain from doing the behavior)

Clear derived his formula from the works of B.J. Fogg and Charles Duhigg. He writes, "Duhigg's book refers to the three steps of the "Habit Loop" as cue, routine, reward. BJ Fogg uses the word trigger instead of cue. And I prefer a reminder since it gives us the memorable "3 R's." Regardless, don't get hung up on the terminology. It's more important to realize that there's a lot of science behind the process of habit formation, and so we can be relatively confident that your habits follow the same cycle, whatever you choose to call it."

I also really like what is said on the Live Bold and Bloom blog by Patrik Edblad from December of 2016. Edblad writes about "Designing Your Environment:"

In many ways, your environment drives your behavior. Have you ever walked into your kitchen, spotted a plate of cookies on the counter, and eaten them just because they were in front of you? If so, you know what I mean. Professor of psychology and bestselling author, Mihaly Csikszentmihalyi, provides an excellent framework to shape your environment to support your desired habits. What he recommends is that you deliberately change the "activation energy" of your habits. The idea is that each one of your habits requires a certain amount of energy to get done. And the more activation energy it needs, the less likely you'll be to follow through and do it. Let's say you want to read more books, but you usually find yourself watching TV instead. What you need to do is:

Decrease the activation energy of your desired habit (reading books). For example, putting a great book next to your living room couch.

Increase the activation energy of your undesired habit (watching TV). For example, putting the TV remote in another room.

By changing the activation energy of your behaviors, you can nudge yourself in the right direction.

Friends, you have so many strategies you can implement to make your new, positive habits stick. I don't even think I've scratched the surface here, but you guys are smart, and you'll figure out where you need to go from here.

You've done it. You've picked up all the tools and learned the strategies to Elevate Your 8. And the rest is up to you. I would love to hear about your wins and "aha" moments as you work your way through this experience.

Please come find me on Facebook at Elevate Your 8; and you email me directly through my website, www.krismcpeak.com

Appendix

Great Resources for Time Management, Productivity, and Other Elevate Your 8 stuff:

Making "Work" Work for You by Kris McPeak

Sleep Smarter by Shawn Stevenson

Anything ever written by Laura Vanderkam

Link to all the downloadable resources that you'll need: www.krismcpeak.com/elevateyour8book

ABOUT THE AUTHOR

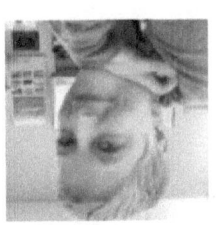

Kris McPeak is the author of "Making 'Work' Work for You", a guide to finding work/life balance; and "The Making 'Work' Work for You Blog Series" of e-books featured on Amazon. She has degrees in Secondary Education and Counselor Education from the University of Arkansas and has worked in higher education for more than 20 years.

Her favorite childhood author was Judy Blume and she currently enjoys the works of Jen Sincero, Laura Vanderkam, Sarah Knight, and Marianne Williamson.

When she's not writing or reading, Kris enjoys swimming and knitting. Kris lives in Southern California with her husband and dog.